Growing Old Disgracefully

How to Upset and Perplex Your Children with Increasingly Erratic and Unreasonable Behavior

Rohan Candappa

Andrews McMeel Publishing

Kansas City

For Leslie and Beulah, Bob and Audrey,
George and Mano, Harry and Eileen,
Barbara and Dennis, Dolly and Michael,
Bobby and Joy, Patrick and Mary,
Susie and Graham, Denzil and Carmen,
and Sunno and Bob.

Thank you for all the things you have
shown me and for all the times you
have shared with me.

04 05 06 07 08 RR2 10 9 8 7 6 5 4 3 2 1

ISBN: 0-7407-4168-3

Library of Congress Control Number: 2004102679

Book design by Lisa Martin

Do not go gentle into that good night,
Old age should burn and rage at close of day;
Rage, rage, against the dying of the light.

—DYLAN THOMAS

You're all doing very well . . .

—YOUNG MR. GRACE

INTRODUCTION

Where's the fun in growing old gracefully? Far better to put your name down for a course of bad behavior, irresponsibility, and questionable fashion choices. And anything that winds your kids up must be worth having a crack at. On top of all that, what better way to keep the Grim Reaper from knocking at your door than having the miserable sod doubled up with laughter?

A simple piece of arithmetic

If life begins at forty, then a sixty-year-old is not yet twenty-one. And think how much mayhem still lay ahead of you at that age. Act accordingly.

Seize the day

If you want to do something, do it. Don't worry if it's right or wrong. Don't worry whether it will work out or not. And above all else, don't worry what other people will think. Especially if their disapproval is based on outdated and insulting pre-conceptions of what age means. So go to those salsa lessons, dye your hair platinum blond, and buy that skimpy skirt.

And as for you ladies . . .

Seizure the day

Faking a heart attack is always a good way of getting some attention or livening up an otherwise dull social occasion.

You're not going out dressed like that!

Remember all that awful stuff that your kids insisted on wearing when they were teenagers? And the grief that you went through whenever they went out looking like an explosion in a garage sale, or an overconfident peacock who took Liberace as a role model, or a juvenile hooker who'd been kicked out of Sodom and Gomorrah for lowering the tone of the neighborhood?

Well, it's payback time.

So the next time you see your children (or better still are staying with
them) it is your solemn duty to fully
explore the sartorial delights of the
wardrobes even Christina Aguilera or
Dennis Rodman rejected as being too
extreme.

You're not going out dressed like that! Some specific advice

Lycra is always a good bet.
Fluorescent Lycra, ideally.

NOBODY LIKES AN OLD FART

The term "old fart" is an offensive phrase usually referring to someone in authority who is set in their ways or lacking a sense of fun. I prefer a much more literal interpretation. What I propose is that you grab the bull by the horns and fart in public as often, and as vociferously, as possible. The chances are that the people around you will excuse your behavior as nothing more than a symptom of some unspecified malaise associated with aging.

What more license do you need to enjoy yourself?

Uncle Stan's Theory of Relativity

This was first expounded by my uncle Stanley. His theory was that, relatively speaking, the older you get, the more annoying your relatives become.

Need hip replacements be so predictable?

Why not make the surgeon really earn his money? If you need a hip replaced, insist on having an elbow put in.

DON'T THINK OF IT AS ABUSE, THINK OF IT AS SATIRE

By the time you retire you will have well and truly earned the right to comment on the collective madness that still grips all the wage slaves that you've left behind. So every now and then go to a bus stop or train station crowded with early morning commuters and force them to contemplate the ludicrous sheeplike nature of their predicament by repeated use of the following phrase:

"Baa-Baa."

How to silence the lambs

The "Baa-Baa" methodology can also be productively employed when confronted by the young lining up to get into the latest "happening" bar, or club, or political/social ideology.

It's slang, innit

Why should impenetrable verbiage
be the sole preserve of the young?
A few suggestions follow.

Hip Hop
Type of dancing attempted by those
who've had one or more of their hips
replaced.

Ford Siesta
Nodding off in the back of a car.

Walkered
Getting so hammered that you need
support to make it home or back to
your own (or ideally someone else's)
bed.

Dis

This is a version of the ghetto slang "dis," which on the street means to "disrespect" someone. In our context, "dis" means something even more dangerous. It means to "disinherit" someone. So, for instance, if your children are not taking enough notice of you, your opinions, or your desires, just hit them with the following line: "Yo, Rugrat, you dis me and I'll dis you!"

TPT

This stands for "Top Plate Tango" and describes the malarkey involved in eating something decidedly denture-unfriendly, e.g., pomegranates.

W. (Pronounced "Double You")
A phrase that applies to the offspring of an acquaintance forced by circumstance or expectation to follow in their parents' footsteps and take over the family business despite no real aptitude for it, e.g., George W. Bush.

Age Rage
A totally justified response to encounters with ageism.

Penile Dementia
The state of confusion that grips certain men (notably lead singers of the Rolling Stones) who've reached an advanced age but still believe their love interests should be young enough to be their daughters.

Celluheavy

And you thought the cellulite of middle age was hard to face.

Wanderbra

Designed to assist ladies blessed with an ample, and once firm, bosom that now wanders off in all directions at every opportunity.

Pro-macassar

Shadowy and elusive (and historically speaking victorious) opposition to the once ubiquitous antimacassar movement.

Youthless

Apt description of attitudes and individuals that place youth at the center of the universe.

Has it ever occurred to you just how much fun a bull can have in a china shop?

Supermarkets and department stores just love arranging their goods in eye-catching displays. And, who can say that as a child they were never tempted to knock over a pyramid of cans? But back then you never really had the nerve to do it because you knew that you'd get "told off by your mother."

The question you've got to ask yourself now is: If you were "inadvertently" to send a painstakingly arranged display tumbling, who's going to tell you off? Indeed, feign extreme regret, spiced up with a dash of doddery old fooldom, after your misdemeanor and you might even score a cup of coffee off of the kindly staff whose display you've just destroyed.

STRANGE HOW THE HORIZON KEEPS MOVING FURTHER AWAY

It is a well-documented fact that old age is always ten to fifteen years older than the age that you are.

That'll confuse the buggers

On a crowded bus or train, make a point of offering your seat to someone obviously much younger than yourself.

A few thoughts on built-in obsolescence (and design classics)

In a society driven by consumerism it seems that we have an insatiable desire for new things. Cars should never be more than a few years old. Fashions should change every season. And computers (for example) seem to go out of date by the time you get them out of the box and have figured out how to turn them on.

The idea of obsolescence is built into what we buy, and buy into, so that we can keep on consuming new stuff. Indeed so enamored are we of consuming new stuff that things that actually do what they're supposed to, and keep on doing what they're supposed to, have to be accorded a status that elevates them above the norm. They become "design classics."

So what has all this got to do with growing older? It's simple. Things may possess built-in obsolescence, but people don't. If the society we live in thinks the opposite, then it is that society itself that is obsolete. And if there is a real design classic out there, it is you and I.

The repairman cometh

Be warned, it's a well-known fact that as you get older there are sketchy repairmen out there who see you as a soft touch.

If someone at the supermarket in a brown corduroy bomber jacket tried to sell you something labeled "The Elixir of Youth," you'd snort a snort of derision and go on your way.

Which is, of course, the exact same response you'd have to a glossy commercial on the television if someone in a white coat tried to sell you something labeled "Anti-Aging Cream," isn't it? (Even if it does come from the Laboratory Ga-Ga.)

THE ONLY ANTI-AGING CREAM THAT REALLY WORKS

A huge chunk of ice cream, ideally old-fashioned vanilla, cut from a block and sandwiched between two flat, rectangular wafers, eaten in the garden on the hottest day of the summer. As it drips all over your hand and your clothes and leaks from the side of your mouth, if you don't feel like an eight-year-old again, then you really are beyond hope.

What's in a name?

So you hit the later years of your life and suddenly you're faced with the age-old dilemma. Namely, what name do you call yourself?

The options are bleak. There's over-the-hill, retiree, sixty-plus, senior citizen, senior, or wrinkly. None of them is in the least appealing as a choice. That's why over the next few pages I'd like to suggest a few alternatives.

LMA

First up is a term that derives from the practice of that oh-so-lovable sector of society, real estate agents. When confronted with trying to sell properties in an area of a city that is less desirable than a neighboring area they, ingeniously, reclassify the offending area as an appendage of the desirable one. So, in the context of this book, I propose that you're no longer old, rather you're enjoying your late middle age. All of which makes you an LMA—a Late Middle Ager.

Beyond Grown-updom

Next is a term that hearkens back to childhood's joyous optimism. Remember when you were a kid and weren't allowed to do the things you wanted to do? Everything would be different, you told yourself, when you were a Grown-up?

Well, now that you've been a Grown-up and have discovered you still aren't allowed to do the things you want to do, maybe you should try the nirvana of being a Grown-old.

Essentially, just as Grown-ups escape the restrictions placed on children, Grown-olds escape the restrictions placed on Grown-ups. Now doesn't that sound fun?

SNDY

The third option is my favorite. It cuts to the chase and cuts through the crap. SNDY: Still Not Dead Yet.

YOU TREAT THIS PLACE LIKE A HOTEL!

Well, how else are you supposed to behave when you go round to stay with your kids? I favor complaining about the accommodation, leaving your shoes out to be polished, and banging on the floor for room service whenever you fancy a snack after midnight.

And don't forget to pinch the bath-robe when you go home.

Or are you just pleased to see me?

This one's a technique for the gentlemen.

When out with friends, bring the conversation around to the amazing effectiveness of Viagra. When your compatriots doubt you, produce a small tablet from your pocket and go off to find some water to take it with. While you're away, remove the large zucchini (or cucumber) that you've secreted in your bag or coat and arrange it appropriately in your underpants.

Return to your compatriots and apologize for the fact that sometimes the tablets don't work as well as they should.

And this one's a technique for the ladies

Visit a sex shop. Buy a vibrating egg. Take it out of its packaging and leave it lying around at home the next time your friends, neighbors, children, or priest comes to visit.

Ask them to help you change the batteries.

Don't think of it as a stair lift; think of it as a monorail

Once again we come up against the problem of perception. So a stair lift is seen both as a badge of infirmity and as a source of sight gags for TV comedians. But look at it another way and what is a stair lift but your very own, private, monorail? And hasn't the monorail long been hailed as the perfect high-tech solution to many of the world's urban transport problems?

Key to my aim of realizing the full potential of the stair lift is the quantum leap of questioning why it should be limited to only going up and down the stairs. Why can't a whole rail network of tracks serve your home? And why should they be designed to take only one passenger at a time?

Indeed, if we're really going to push the envelope on stair lift design, why not get the good people who make them to confer with roller coaster designers from Walt Disney World and come up with a track layout heavy on the "wow" factor. Do this and you'll not only have turned the stair lift from a bit of a joke into an outstanding local tourist attraction that has kids lining up around the block, but you'll also soon be able to pay off your initial investment by charging people for the ride.

HOW TO STRETCH PEOPLE'S PATIENCE

In supermarkets pretend that you can't reach items stacked on the top shelves. Ask a customer who is obviously in a hurry to stretch up for you and get one down. Then, when they give you the item, decide you don't want it and ask them (ever so sweetly) if they could put it back.

Why should teens have all the fun?

Teenagers are generally frowned upon by respectable society because of the way they dress, think, don't fit in with conventions, and seem to be leading a life of rootless laziness, aimlessness, and fun at everyone else's expense. They're also experts at kicking up a fuss about issues to which they object.

That's why I suggest that it's high time we instigated the phenomenon of Old-agers who would adopt a similarly admirable attitude to life.

A GREAT WAY TO
OUTFLANK YOUR CHILDREN

Form a strategic alliance with your
grandchildren. Then deploy your
forces in a classic pincer movement
to outmaneuver your enemy.

There's no statute of limitations on memories of misdemeanors

When your children have their own children, nothing causes as much irritation as undermining their authority. So when your grandchildren are old enough to understand, there's much fun to be had by regaling them with stories of all the trouble that their parents got into.

Soon you'll be safe in the knowledge that the next time your grandkids are being told off by their parents for some particular naughtiness the following lovely wail will fill the air: "But Granddad/Grandma says you used to do it!"

Presents tense

There's also a great deal you can achieve by buying your grandchildren presents that their parents have sensibly refused to buy for them.

The biter bit

A set of secondhand false teeth is always a useful prop to take along to a dreaded lunch or dinner engagement. It takes but a little imagination to generate all manner of mayhem with said gnashers during the meal. My own favorite technique is to conceal the dentures in your hand, feign a coughing fit, raise your hand politely to cover the coughs, then as a particularly violent spasm grips you, fling the teeth across the room.

For added amusement try to get the teeth to land in the plate of whichever of your mealtime companions has been the most boring.

A prank to pull if you're feeling particularly mischievous

Borrow a cane. Go out on the streets and stand patiently by the edge of a pedestrian crossing. When a kindly motorist stops to let you cross, totter, painfully slowly, across the road, using the cane as an obviously much-needed support. The kindly motorist will no doubt be watching you, forced to contemplate the physical frailties that lie ahead for so many of us. Two-thirds of the way across the crossing, snatch up the cane and sprint the rest of the way and off into the distance, laughing.

Welcome to your anecdotage

Entering your anecdotage can really be one of the most rewarding parts of getting older. Your aim should be to bore all those around you with stories about incidents and events that they have no interest in and, ideally, occurred long before they were born. The real skill, however, lies in selecting "interesting" memories that are incredibly dull and "funny" stories totally devoid of even an iota of humor, but still recounting them as if they are the most fascinating events in the history of the universe.

For added fun, invest in a stopwatch and set it going as you start your anecdote. Stop timing when you spot the first pair of eyes in your audience glazing over. Then the next time you play, try and lower your personal best time.

Aunty social behavior

This is the overly affectionate and totally inappropriate behavior pattern adopted in public by aging aunts that make long–since grown-up nieces and nephews cringe with embarrassment.

Please indulge in this at every possible opportunity.

A SUREFIRE TECHNIQUE FOR WINDING UP YOUR DAUGHTER- OR SON-IN-LAW

Nothing beats subtly criticizing the way that your children are bringing up their children.

Heart bypass

This is an admirable event that occurs later on in life when you come to the conclusion that society is increasingly unable to deal with real emotions but instead promotes overwrought sentimental drivel in their place. Prime examples of this include the over-the-top orchestrations of grief associated with national disasters, the response of spoiled brats (of all ages and political parties) when they don't get their own way, and any TV program featuring crying celebrities and Barbara Walters.

Existential aunts

This is a corruption of the phrase "existential angst," though corruption may be too derogatory a word, as I believe that in many ways existential aunts are the ultimate practitioners of existential angst.

With an existential aunt, the philosophy of existentialism that concerns itself with the lack of any in-built meaning or purpose in the universe collides with the aunty school of behavior, in which the aunt worries unduly about how their niece or nephew is doing at school, comments on how much they've grown, and gives pathetically small gifts of money on birthdays or at Christmas.

In practice, existential aunts say things like, "If you're going out, make sure you dress warmly and wear a scarf because it's freezing out there and our existence is essentially meaningless."

As you get older, remodeling yourself as an existential aunt provides great opportunity for both concerning and confusing your nieces and nephews.

A ludicrously easy way to impress people with your vigor and vitality

Forget high-energy diets. Forget rigorous exercise routines. Forget plastic surgery. Instead, when meeting new people, tell them you're fifteen years older than you actually are.

PLASTIC SURGERY: A MORE ECONOMICAL (AND MORE EASILY REVERSIBLE) APPROACH

Why waste thousands on procedures with uncertain results when a decent roll of duct tape can be had for less than a few dollars?

Over the hill—a re-evaluation

It's all a question of attitude. I mean, deconstruct the phrase and it reveals itself not to be so derogatory.

Climbing the hill is generally hard work. Being on top of the hill, I admit, does provide a sense of achievement and a great view. Then after that you come down the hill, which is relatively easy and enjoyable. And then you find yourself at the bottom of the hill on level land.

In my experience this is where things get really interesting. And they get really interesting because you are confronted with choices. All the time you're doing all that hill work you're kind of locked into a course of action. You have to go up the hill, you have to look around at the top of it, you have to come down it. But now that you're "over the hill" it's up to you what happens next.

Do you wander round the flat bit you're on, having fun? Do you set out in search of another hill? Do you, having done a hill, decide you'd like to have a go at a mountain? Or do you give yourself the challenge of exploring all the other geographical features that are out there? Like lakes? And rivers? And glaciers? And canyons?

Look at things this way and it soon becomes clear just how small-minded and pathetic all those people are who have the nerve to think of you, patronizingly, as being "over the hill." After all, they're still stuck on the bloody hill. And they labor under the severely deluded misconception that the hill is all that life has to offer.

Gullible's Travels

As retirement looms, your children will probably start asking you what you plan to do with all the extra time that stretches out before you. Tell them that you've always planned to do a bit of traveling to see a few places. Then wait till they've exclaimed that this is a great idea and hit them with a list of countries so dangerous that even Christiane Amanpour would shake her head and claim that the dog had eaten her passport.

A reintroduction to one of the long-lost pleasures to be experienced in bed

For this one you have to wait until it's winter. Then wait for an evening when those bizarre oracles of meteorology with the strange hand-waving actions predict a "heavy frost tonight." Then turn off your central heating. Then go up to your bedroom, remove the duvet that's on the bed, and replace it with the sheet and blankets that you've invested in for this delicious saunter down Memory Lane.

Half an hour before you go to bed, boil the teapot and fill your other recent purchase—the hot-water bottle. Place the hot-water bottle in the bed.

When it's time to retire, brush your teeth in the now-freezing bathroom. Get changed in the seemingly even colder bedroom. Then climb into your bed and sink back into a sea of sensations that will have the memories flooding back.

Note: Make sure that the stopper is in the hot-water bottle properly, or it won't just be a sea of sensations you'll be sinking back into.

And here's another reason why we should regard the creeping duvetization of the world with suspicion

The problem is that your grandchildren are growing up at a time when, if they're asked to write a poem about snow* in elementary school, they will find themselves having to say that "snow duveted the ground." All because they've never encountered a blanket in their life.

I mean is this really the kind of world we want to live in?

*All children are asked this as it's always been part of the unofficial national curriculum, just like writing about what you did during the holidays or having to watch a fat boy/girl cry during P.E.

ONE OF THE PUZZLING IRONIES ASSOCIATED WITH AGING

Even though you, as an individual, have long since stopped growing, you will find that your underwear hasn't. The older you are, the bigger it gets.

Will Power

Never underestimate the strength of your Will Power. But remember that in the context of getting older, Will Power has nothing to do with your desire and drive to do something. Instead, it is the power that the writing and, more importantly, threatened rewriting of your will gives you over your children and relatives.

Throwing a spaniel in the works

At Christmas buy your grandchildren a puppy, having made certain not to clear it with their parents first. And if you do have more than one grand-child it's probably best that they get one puppy each. After all, it's only fair.

Game Boy

Buy a handheld electronic game console. Make sure you've set the volume control to maximum. Pull the game from your pocket and start playing it at the most inappropriate moments. For example, while you're in church. Or during a trip to the theater. Or while your partner is trying to have a conversation with you.

Game Boy, advanced

Or while your partner is trying to make love to you.

As your salad days are over, you may as well order fries

There is a time in a person's youth that has been described as their "salad days." It is characterized as a period in which they are innocent, naive, and inexperienced. So it only seems fair that at the other end of your own personal time line there should also be a food-based analogy that profoundly captures some universal truth about your life.

My best shot is that as the clock runs down every person enters a period of their life known as their "steak and potatoes days." It is a period I characterize as one in which you are no

longer innocent, naive, and inexperienced and so always order exactly
what you want in restaurants and
(metaphorically speaking) in the
restaurant of life.

ASHES TO ASHES

Invest in a small urn. Fill it with the ashes of some disposable item you've burned on a bonfire. Then the next time unsuspecting friends, relatives, or neighbors visit your home, position the urn in such a place that they will inevitably knock it over and spill the contents while you are out of the room. Then sit back and enjoy the show.

More ashes to ashes

Again invest in a small urn. Again fill it with ashes. Then dress up in your best dark suit and take the urn, and the ashes, out with you to scatter them in their final resting place. Choose a location and a time that are highly inappropriate, for example, on the platform of a busy train station in the middle of the morning rush hour. Or in a church yard just as a photographer is arranging the group picture of a wedding. Or in your neighbors' back garden when they're having a barbecue.

Digging up the hatchet

Over the course of your life you have probably been involved in many disputes. They may have been over work, or love, or family matters or any number of other things. Being the sensible person that you are, you no doubt realized that if a satisfactory resolution wasn't to be had the best thing to do would be to let the matter go and get on with your life.

Well, now's the time to jettison all that namby-pamby forgive-and-forget nonsense and sort the matter out once and for all. And if you don't fancy the prospect of a confrontation in person, then just send a letter with the simple, reassuring, unsigned message "I haven't forgiven you."

Then you can move on. And you'll be safe in the knowledge that your old adversary will have to, at the very least, spend some time contemplating all the people they've screwed over in their life.

After all, don't the Sicilians say "Revenge is a dish best served cold"? (Which makes revenge a dish very similar to gazpacho.)

SOMETHING TO CHEW OVER

Much fun can be had by always offering taffy to friends with false teeth.

A brief lesson in semantics (or how the meanings of words change the older you get)

When you were growing up, having a secure home life was a good thing, while having a sheltered home life had many negative connotations. Now that you're growing old, however, "sheltered" accommodation is the good thing, while living in "secure" accommodation basically means that you've been locked up.

My point is this: The meanings of words change. So you've got to keep on your toes and have your wits about you. And look suspiciously upon anything that your nearest and dearest ask you to sign.

Briefs encounter

Passion doesn't disappear as the years pass. It's more that its nature changes, and the opportunities to act upon the impulses that seize us have to battle against the inertia of habit and convention. And all too often fear of what others will think acts as the most overzealous of chaperones.

Which is a shame, because in the words of the old song, "a little of what you fancy does you good."

But be warned, because when you do carpe the diem and succumb to the delights of a blood-pumpingly passionate bit of groping and grappling, there will come the Briefs Encounter Moment. This is the moment when you're stopped in your tracks by the sobering thought that if things do go any further you will have to reveal the full horror, scope, scale, and general demeanor of the underwear that you are wearing.

THE WISDOM OF THE ANCIENTS

One of the benefits of getting older is that for some obscure reason there lingers around the peripheries of most societies the quasi-folkloric idea that the old can be very wise. Frankly, this is too good an opportunity to miss. That's because it provides you with a license to talk drivel, dressed up in profundity.

To help you with this exercise I've put down a few suggestions of my own. But the most fun is to be had by making the things up for yourself.

The wisdom of the ancients— a few examples

1. It is easier for a rich man to needle a camel by poking him in the eye than it is for a fat man to get into the Kingdom of Leather.

2. If trees were made of cheese, then owls would live in Gouda.

3. Where there's muck, there's someone who's really let their standards slip.

4. If the fire wasn't hot, how on earth would we cook the porridge?

5. The movement you need is on your shoulder.

(Okay, so I admit I didn't make that last one up, but nicked it from "Hey Jude." But I've always had no idea what it means. So I thought I'd stick it in on the off chance that Sir Paul would read it and get in touch.)

You're not getting old, you're investigating Chaos Theory

Chaos Theory is one of the real hot potatoes in the world of super-intellectual, ivory-towered scientists who rack their brains and run the world's megacomputers ragged trying to explain the true nature of the cosmos. Chaos Theory states that even the most basic rules can occasionally behave in totally unpredictable ways.

So when one morning you get up and find that the simple task of getting dressed has suddenly become complicated due to creaking limbs, aching joints, or failing eyesight, don't put it down to aging. Put it down to Chaos Theory.

Indeed, put together a decent proposal and you might even be able to con some cash out of the government so that you can further your research.

AN EASY WAY TO SAY "HI" TO THE PASSING WORLD

Eschew conventional pot plants like geraniums and petunias when deciding what to place in your windows. Instead cultivate real pot plants. Marijuana is both decorative and useful. And should the local police ask about your horticultural selections, explain that you are merely making early preparations for the onset of glaucoma.

The joy of slacks

There will come a point in your life when the wearing of slacks will start to appeal much more. Embrace the moment and incorporate the philosophy implicit in the name of that garment into your lifestyle. "Slacks" derives from "slack," a word meaning "not tight, taut, tense, or busy." What a great way to live.

Babbling On

Babbling On is one of the true pleasures of attaining a venerable age. It
is a skill that is easily achieved and
that is infinitely adaptable to almost
any set of circumstances. What you
need to do is find a topic that you
know very little about, then talk
about it for as long as possible.

Indeed, in the ideal Babbling On
scenario, the amount of knowledge
possessed should be in precise inverse
proportion to the length of conversation attempted. And now that I come
to think of it, "conversation" is the
wrong word. A well-honed Babbling

On session should at all times attempt to become a monologue. And better still, a monologue that wears the demeanor of a lecture.

Probably the best setting for Babbling On is a long car journey.

Coffee shop fun

Look, it's their own fault. I mean you go into a coffee shop wanting a simple cup of coffee and suddenly you're confronted with more choices than the pope on an official visit to Denmark where a rather over-elaborate smorgasbord has been laid out for lunch.

Well, this is how you can get your own back.

What you do is peer up at the long list of coffee options so proudly pro-claimed on the signage on the wall and, one by one, ask what they are. At the end of each description say

"Oh, that sounds nice," pause as if you're about to order what's just been described, then apologetically ask about the next coffee on the list.

Carry on until all the coffees have been described, then throw the whole situation back in the lap of the counter staff by feigning confusion and asking them what they think you should have.

Ponder their suggestion for a minute, then with a mildly triumphant little sigh say, "I know, I'll have a nice cup of tea."

Game, set, and match to you, I think.

The problem with walkers

Look, I realize that the prospect of walkerdom is probably off in the dim and distant, but I think that's precisely why we should consider the wretched things now. That way we can turn the walker from an object of ridicule into a much-sought-after lifestyle statement as coveted as the latest Fendi bag or Mac laptop.

Up until now, walkers were thought of only in functional terms. Their design was purely utilitarian.

Hence the current walkers look like nothing more than a very basic scaffolding construction, which, while setting the walkee free mobility-wise, also, and somewhat ironically, imprisons them in a perceptual cage of infirmity.

Clearly what's needed is a radical re-imagination of the damned thing.

I mean, what would a walker designed by Phillipe Starck look like? Or one that had been subject to the magical eye of John Galliano? Or what about Damien Hirst? What would a Damien Hirst walker look like? Now wouldn't that have all the Sunday papers clamoring to get the "New Walkers" on the front of their magazines?

So in this brave new world the walker would not be stigmatized, but would be the subject of waiting lists at the most exclusive of boutiques. And potential purchasers would have to prove their infirmity even to get in to see the latest walker collections from Paris and Milan.

"Regrets, I've had a few"

Who's Frank kidding? We've all got regrets. Loads of 'em. And if we really think we've got "too few to mention," it's more likely a case that we can't remember all the stupid things we've done in our life, or all the bad decisions we've made.

After all, wasn't it the French existentialist Albert Camus who wrote (in French obviously) "A man without regrets is like a grapefruit without a grapefruit knife"?

Anyway, my point is that the only thing worth really regretting is having no regrets. Indeed, it is my profound belief that regrets should be got out and agonized over at regular intervals. That's because regrets can help give a patina of depth to your life. They enable you to say to yourself, "Look, I'm not a shallow person because in my life I've made bad decisions and suffered because of them."

And it's vitally important that you share these regrets with your nearest and dearest as frequently as possible. Boy, will that wind them up.

A couple of examples follow.

I should have married someone else

This is a fantastic regret to throw into the mix at the appropriate moment. It conjures up images of long-lost love, long-suffering marriage, and the worrying implication that your children are somehow not quite up to scratch.

I was a real high-flyer

Primarily a tactic to be employed by the older woman. The essence of it is that you gave up a more-than-promising career in order to look after your kids. To add a real subtle twist of the knife to this ploy, whenever the subject comes up, look a little wistful and say in a soft voice, "No, of course I don't regret it."

That's guaranteed to generate guilt trips of the highest order in your children. What bliss.

It's not the silence of the lambs that's the real horror story, it's the groaning of the limbs

So you used to spring out of bed every morning, but now you're more likely to wake up having felt every spring. Unfortunately aching limbs come with the territory of age. Of course, there are various sensible things you can do to ease the situation. You can change your diet. You can start exercising. You can buy a new bed. Or you can initiate an illicit affair with someone totally inappropriate so that every morning you're too busy making love, or too racked with guilt, to notice your aching limbs.

Not that hard a decision, is it?

HEE-HAW, HA-HA

Let it be known to your nearest and dearest that (being of sound mind and body) you're giving serious consideration to the matter of your will. Then casually leave lying around brochures for a donkey sanctuary.

A BRIEF NOTE ON
THE HAIRPIECE VIRUS

This is an odd little rascal that can affect the mind of an older person. While this may sound a tad perturbing, the actual affliction caused is so specific and benign that little or no research has been conducted into finding a cure or a treatment. Essentially the hairpiece virus exclusively affects people who wear bad wigs and makes them think that nobody knows.

Generation Vex

This is a phrase derived from the 1990s term "Generation X" describing a generation of young people disaffected, directionless, and having no part to play in society. It's a situation with which many older people can identify.

Generation Vex is a response to this disagreeable state of affairs. As in you don't have to sit there and just accept the role society has mapped out for you. You can complain. And you should complain. Especially when you find yourself defined and delimited by other people's preconceived ideas of what age means.

The age of enlightenment or the age for a light enema?

One of the most perplexing things you can do as far as your children are concerned is to embrace the pleasures of alternative medicine. Which is why it's a great prank to pretend that you have. The sketchier the treatment you purport to be indulging in, the better. You know the kind of thing—jojoba and tofu body rubs, boll weevil extract dietary supplements, and any exercise regime that involves you standing in the garden in the early morning wearing only your underpants.

The Holy Grail of all this misleading of your offspring is to convince them of the benefits of colonic irrigation to such an extent that they try it for themselves. Especially if you've never actually had a vacuum shoved up your nether regions yourself. What fun.

Last chance for a midlife crisis

If you didn't have one during your midlife (traditionally when you hit forty), then it really is about time you had one now. If you don't, then you will have missed out on one of life's great opportunities to create stress and concern for those who really care about you. And you will also have missed out on the license to behave badly that is usually extended to those enjoying a midlife crisis.

In its classic manifestation a midlife crisis revolves around the realization that the career that you've invested so much time and effort in is in the doldrums and no longer satisfying, as is (or so you imagine) your marriage and your relationship with your children. So you look around for some totally inappropriate way in which to rebel.

Described in these terms it's easy to see why hitting sixty-plus and realizing that you haven't had a midlife crisis is rather like finding an old savings bond in a drawer that has long ago matured that you can still cash in.

Typical options for Late-Midlife-Crisis-induced bad behavior include having an affair with someone much younger, "investing" in plastic surgery, buying a Harley-Davidson, and opting out of all the choices and beliefs and obligations that once delimited your life.

Now if you can't have fun with those, then you're not really trying.

Drug abuse: how an aging population can help

Youth isn't the only thing wasted on the young. Drugs are, too. I mean there you are in the first blossom, lust roaming your underpants like a mouse in a cheese factory, with all of life's petty disillusionments still way off in the distance, and that's when you're supposed to experiment with mind-altering substances.

For instance, why take a drug that has you talking a mile a minute, convinced of the all-conquering importance of your ego, when you're young enough to jabber like an idiot unaided and have an ego that's almost impossible to inflate any further?

And why puff on the old joint in order to help you "chill out, man" when you know nothing of, for example, tax returns, estate agents, marital disharmony, or bosses young enough to be your kids?

Wind the clock on half a century, however, and the case for a little something that blissfully alters the consciousness every now and again is hard to argue against.

After all, it's not as if you run the risk of screwing up your future. Or that drugs won't feature heavily in the years to come. You'll have drugs for your heart, for your blood, for your mind, for your bladder, and any-where else your body decides to kick up a fuss. So why not throw in a few drugs to make you feel good, too?

Picture the scene. Christmas dinner at one of your children's houses. The TV's on full blast. As are the arguments. And the Playstations. And it's twenty past two but lunch is still at least an hour away because someone forgot to defrost the turkey. And then little Persephone decides to throw up over the shih tzu because she's guzzled all the chocolate decorations off the tree. But you, oblivious to it all, are drifting off in the mellowest of mellow hazes. All thanks to that hand-rolled little fella filled with "Granddad/Grandma's special 'baccy."

So let's have mandatory life sentences for anyone selling or supplying drugs to the young, but grant licenses to anyone supplying to the more mature, deserving, and appreciative consumer. And why not scrap Social Security and provide ready-rolled, quality-controlled joints of an equivalent value at post offices instead?

Now who could possibly object to that?

"HE'S IN HIS SHED"

Incidentally, that last piece on drugs lends a whole new dimension to the attractions of a "potting" shed.

A whole new approach to the Seven Deadly Sins

1. Sloth

2. Avarice

3. Envy

4. Lust

5. Anger

6. Gluttony

7. Pride

Think of it as a checklist of things to do.

"We're all going on a summer vacation . . . "

No more worries for a week or two? Oh really?

Never underestimate the fun to be had by going on vacation with your children's family. After all, on what other occasion would you find yourself with so many new places, experiences, and things to complain about?

And you don't even have to wait to get to your vacation destination to get the stress-inducing ball rolling. For example, if you're flying, you can insist on getting to the airport a good two and a half hours before check-in time "just to be on the safe side." Or if you're traveling by car, "Are we there yet?" is too irritating a question just to be left to your grand-children.

When you do get to wherever you're staying, in response to the inevitable question "Do you like it?" pause just long enough to plant a seed of doubt, then say, "It's very nice." But subse-quently drop subtle hints that you're not keen on the room, the view, the other tourists, the locals, the weather, and indeed the place you're visiting.

Then go on a vain hunt for a "decent cup of tea." And report back with your findings. It's also worthwhile forgetting to take along a book to read and then borrowing the one brought by your son- or daughter-in-law. But for added spice remember to take along a copy of the weekly *TV Guide* from home. And every evening regale your companions with all your "favorite" shows that you're missing by being away.

Then on your last night get completely plastered on some vile-tasting liqueur and end up kissing someone you shouldn't on the dance floor of the local disco, leaving your kids to drag you off saying, "If we don't go now, we'll miss the plane!"

After all, isn't that what you had to do with them all those years ago?

Line cutting

It's really annoying when some cocky jerk of a youth arrogantly shoves their way to the front of the line where you, and others, have been waiting patiently. Unsurprisingly, it would be just as annoying if you, as someone old enough to know better, did the same. So lose your inhibitions and give it a go.

The Gap Year

This is another concept wasted on the young. Essentially it's a year off between high school and going on to college. The idea is that the callow youth in question broadens their horizons, sees a bit of the world, gains some independence, and lets their hair down before they get mired in the serious business of study. It should also involve much drinking, carousing, and inappropriate sexual shenanigans. (Just so long as the parents don't find out.)

Which is all well and good but why should this Gap Year thing (which in my day was either not an option or had the slightly different name of "screwing around") be only available to the young, who have, frankly, done very little to deserve it? That's why I propose that in between the day you retire and the day you actually start your retirement, you too should be entitled to head off on a Gap Year.

The idea is that the not-so-callow individual in question broadens their horizons, sees a bit of the world, gains some independence, and lets what's left of their hair down before they get mired in the serious business of retirement. It should also involve much drinking, carousing, and inappropriate sexual shenanigans. (Just so long as the children don't find out.)

Is it just me, or is small print getting smaller?

No, it's not getting smaller. So stop being so vain and get yourself some decent glasses.

Been there, done that, got the T-shirt

This is a conversational ploy that is particularly effective in annoying anyone younger than yourself. Whenever said younger person is talking about any particular experience that they've recently experienced, good, bad, or indifferent, hit them with this phrase.

By doing so you will be letting them know, not too subtly, that whatever they've done, enjoyed, or lived through, you did it all first and, hence, their experiences are in no way original and, double hence, somehow less valid and, triple hence, their life is about as interesting as a repeat of *Touched by an Angel*.

A trip down mammary lane (for the ladies)

This involves a stint in front of the mirror lamenting how it's not only governments with large majorities that seem to lose shape, firmness, and direction as time goes on.

A trip down mammary lane (for the gentlemen)

This involves a walk outside on a hot summer's day when, in the words of the old song, "June is busting out all over," and so are all her friends. And the realization strikes you that you've completely forgotten what a certain part of the opposite sex's anatomy feels like.

Wrinkly: how to reclaim, redefine, and defuse abuse

Some people think that the best way to deal with verbal abuse is to rise above it. My preferred approach is to undermine it. Just like Cyrano de Bergerac did that time when someone foolishly mocked his big nose. So if the term "wrinkly" does come your way, throw it straight back and suggest one of the following self-deprecating yet self-empowering alternatives instead.

Shrinkly
An older person who finds themselves somewhat diminished in stature

Thinkly

Anyone over sixty who spends a lot of time thinking about profound and important stuff

Sprinkly

Any compatriot afflicted by incontinence

Crinkly

Old, but in the delightful position of being in possession of lots of the folding stuff

Drinkly

Those who indulge in the occasional nip at every possible opportunity

Pinkly

An individual who still holds to a left-wing or Marxist analysis of life

Pinkly

Alternatively, someone both gray and gay

Winkly

People who see no reason why age should be a barrier to flirting

Kinkly

People who see no reason why age should be a barrier to an, let's just say, "imaginative" approach to sex

Nodding off

Now this is one of the true delights
to be had in the Gorgeous Garden of
Getting On. Basically, you're allowed
to nod off. So whenever, for example,
you're bored out of your skull by the
mindless inanity of the conversation
your family is pursuing around the
table after Sunday lunch, just drop
your chin onto your chest, let your
eyelids droop, and pretend to fall
asleep.

Your family, bless them, will think
that you're "tired." But little will they
suspect that what you're really tired
of is them.

The wine and cheese analogy of aging

Wine improves with age. As does cheese. But both have to be stored in a cool place to do so. In many ways we possess similar qualities to both cheese and wine. That's why heading off somewhere hot and sunny to spend your retirement may not have the hoped-for effect.

After all, while a ripe Camembert may be a thing of beauty, one that's completely melted in the heat and run off down the cheese board, down the legs of the dining table, and out into the night in search of a cab isn't the sort of thing you want to be confronted by every time you look in the bathroom mirror.

"ARE YOU LOOKING AT ME?" (AS ROBERT DE NIRO ONCE SO SUCCINCTLY PUT IT)

Get together with a group of fellow compatriots of a similar age and hang around on street corners smoking cigarettes and kicking an empty beer can about. Don't move aside when anyone under the age of twenty tries to get past. For added menace turn up the collar on your parka. (And turn down the volume on your hearing aid.)

Remember the days when Donald Trump was famous for being a billionaire?

For gentlemen most of whose hair has long since decided it's time to vacate headquarters, the most sensible option is to wear what's left in a short, well-groomed arrangement. Growing it long and then brushing it sideways, or indeed forward, in a vain attempt to cover up an otherwise bald pate fools nobody and can only result in furtive hilarity among all those who see it. For this reason it is imperative that you adopt the Homer Simpson at the earliest possible opportunity. Think of it less as a hairstyle and more as a chance to spread a little light relief among the youthful masses who lead such dull and dreary lives that they're desperate for even the smallest diversion to smile about.

Home alone? Then why not home a loan?

In the movie *Home Alone* the child actor Macaulay Culkin, left behind (accidentally) by his parents, thwarts a bunch of adult burglars intent on stripping his home of all its valuable assets.

To the unenlightened viewer it is nothing more than a lightweight bit of slapstick fun. But take a more philosophical stance and what is revealed is a far profounder critique of the way society treats the disenfranchised.

Recast Macaulay's role as that of an older person, left behind not by his parents but his adult children, then reimagine these adult children as the burglars, and *Home Alone* becomes a searing indictment of the way that your children abandon you in a house you worked all your life to buy, then can't wait for you to pop your clogs so that they can sell the place and make a killing.

But the true genius of *Home Alone* is in its title, a title that suggests a solution to the predicament. Namely, take a loan out against the value of your home and blow the cash before your offspring can get their mitts on it.

And that's why *Home Alone* is a masterpiece and a far better and more relevant analysis of aging than even *King Lear*.

Beware the Grayhouse Effect

The dangers of the Greenhouse Effect are well documented. You get increased solar absorption by the atmosphere. Temperatures rise across the globe. The polar ice caps melt. And before you know it they're building exclusive marinas halfway up Mount Everest.

In comparison, the Grayhouse Effect is hardly known at all, but can be just as destructive. You'll encounter it whenever you visit the home of a graying contemporary and notice that they keep their central heating on so high that, for instance, the bathroom isn't prone to the odd spot of mold, but large expanses of mangrove swamp.

The net result for those who live in such conditions is that while they appear to thrive while in their homes, once they step outside they shiver and shrivel like a lizard in a blizzard.

WE REJECTED THE nanny STATE, SHOULDN'T WE DO THE SAME FOR THE GRANny STATE?

The Granny State presupposes that anyone who is a grandmother has to act in certain, granny-like ways. They must have kindly faces and outlooks, they must knit and wear cardigans, and they must be mildly shocked at the goings-on of youngsters. And, of course, they must never have sex. Or even think about it.

What rubbish.

A few alternative granny role models follow.

V.G.

This stands for Vegas Granny. Let's just say she is a female contemporary who's old enough to know better, dress better, and act better. The Vegas Granny wears dresses that are cut too low, heels that are way too high, and, on an evening out, has aims and tactics that are decidedly below the belt. Hence she is a fantastic role model for growing old disgracefully.

The Ethics Granny

At the other end of the spectrum of grannydom from the Vegas Granny is the Ethics Granny.

The Ethics Granny objects to everything. For ethical reasons. Ethical reasons that she expounds loud and clear at every possible opportunity. Especially when in the company of her children.

The Tranny Granny

This is an approach for the more adventurous-minded woman. Basically you decide late on in the game that cross-dressing is the lifestyle option that you feel most comfortable with. Give no word of warning, nor explanation, just turn up one day at your children's houses dressed as a man.

That should set the cat among the canaries.

The Fussing Granny

This is a granny who spreads mild
annoyance and minor irritation by
fussing around all the time. Key
phrases to be used include "Now
where did I put my glasses?" "Oooh,
did I leave the light on in the hall?"
and "Now tell me, dear, which part
of my body do you think I should
get pierced next?"

The N.Y. Granny

By far the best category of granny. The original role model hails from Manhattan. They boast a similar attitude to life as the Vegas Granny, but with a better dress sense. And a more direct approach to the things they want. As in "Grab yer coat, toy-boy, you've scored an old gal."

BIRDS DO IT, BEES DO IT (EVEN CREAKING OLD FARTS DO IT)

Sex is another one of those things that's too much fun to be left to the young. And just because a lot of water may have passed under several of your bridges doesn't mean you can't still have a fair bit of fun splashing around in a boat, if you catch my drift.

What follows are just a few suggestions.

Consult the Calmer Sutra

This is a collection of sexual positions from the East devised for those who, in matters connected with hanky-panky, are still interested in the panky side of things but find that they need to cut down on the hanky end of it all.

Positions featured include the Dromedary (one hump), the Tethered Walker (light bondage), the Drooping Palm (don't worry, it happens to everyone), and the Gushing Well (far too rude to even attempt to explain).

Dressing up

One of the commonest fantasies. For the older man the fantasy usually involves having their partners dress up as Catholic-style schoolgirls, or nurses, or Sophia Loren on a hot day. (Like that's ever going to happen.)

For the older woman the fantasy usually involves having their partner dress up in a clean pair of unbaggy underwear. (Like that's ever going to happen.)

Another common fantasy

Another common fantasy for men of a certain age and social background involves the wearing of hosiery, suspenders, and high-heel shoes. But, hey, ladies, as long as they don't put runs in your panty hose or break the heels of your shoes, my advice is, why not let your partners wear the stuff? Indeed, encouraging them to pursue their "hobby" is a great way of increasing your wardrobe.

Rubberware

Now here's a fetish that we really should encourage older people to get into. After all, there is a potential dual benefit. First, there's sexual gratification. Secondly, if incontinence ever does become a problem in later life, you're ahead of the game in terms of clothing.

Strip teas

For this you need cucumber sand-
wiches, scones, strawberry jam, and
a pot of Earl Grey. You also need to
invite someone over for tea. Then as
the comestibles are consumed you
gradually remove your clothing. How
far you go and what you get up to
are entirely up to you.

Cream teas

Like strip teas, but a far squidgier
encounter.

HRTs

Similar to strip teas and cream
teas, but with a renewed zest for life,
reinvigorated hair, and a glowing
complexion.

"It's the brand-new geegaw that can access the whatsit, and has shedloads of thingummy"

If new technology makes you feel stupid, then you're missing the point. That's because the whole point of new technology is to make you feel stupid. That way the manufacturers know that when the next new technology arrives you'll probably buy that, too, in the vain hope that it's easier to understand.

But, for the older person, there is an upside to this madness. This is the fact that while you may find it hard to come to grips with the intricacies of the new technologies, so do your children. But seeing as they are much younger than you, and kid themselves that they are at one with this rapidly changing world, they will feel that they should understand it all.

So invest in the latest geegaw, get everything out of the box and jumble it up a bit, then take it around to your son or son-in-law's place and ask them to help you sort it out. Then sit back and enjoy the show.

You should be in line for at least a good couple of hours' entertainment, especially the ten minutes at the end when your grandson or granddaughter gets back from school and sets it all up without even looking at the instructions.

A Proustian interlude

Proust, in his magnum opus *À la recherche du temps perdu,* apparently only had to taste a Madeleine and all kinds of memories came flooding back from earlier years. When I first heard this I quickly sought out the book only to be sorely disappointed to discover that the Madeleine in question was a cake and not a character.

But Proust was making a very good point. The taste of something from our childhood or youth can easily reveal a room full of memories. So what is your equivalent of Proust's Madeleines?

Is it the fried chicken you used to eat at your aunt's house for Sunday dinner? Or the tongue-blackening delights of a piece of licorice? Or is it the Spam fritters they used to serve every Thursday at school?

The thing to do is to track them down and try them. And see what memories come flooding back.

Then again there is always the possibility that the taste that you most long for is the taste of a Madeleine. Or a Margaret. Or a Michael. Or a Malcolm. In which case re-creating the sensation might be somewhat harder to achieve.

The Caterpillar Theory

Everyone knows that people are living longer, healthier lives these days. Yet at the same time everyone seems to accept the fact that society has inexorably shifted its focus and its center of power from the old to the young. This makes no sense at all.

If you want an analogy from the world of nature, it's as if caterpillars were to suddenly adopt the ethos that being a caterpillar was the be all, and end all, of everything. Hence the retreat into a cocoon and the subsequent emergence with wings must come as quite a considerable shock. Indeed so great a surprise is it that they may well spend their time crawling around still trying to be caterpillars. Which is rather stupid.

After all, the best thing to do with a pair of wings is to take to the air and fly.

And you thought cell phones were a pain in the ass

Get yourself a cell phone, but make sure it's got a hands-free kit with it. Then put it away in a cupboard until you need it. And when you need it will be that fateful day when you discover that you've started to talk to yourself in public.

Under these circumstances, retrieve your phone, fit the earpiece, and hit the streets. Now you can be secure in the knowledge that nobody will suspect that you're talking to yourself—they'll just think that you're "on your cell."

A VERY GOOD REASON TO WEAR TOO MUCH MAKEUP

It'll really embarrass your children.

nostalgia isn't what it used to be

Nostalgia was so much better in the old days. But now it's almost a case of last month's hype being this month's nostalgia. What the concept of nostalgia needs is a good kick in the backside.

Some new categories would be a good starting point.

nicestalgia

This involves sitting around, drinking tea and eating cakes, discussing how much nicer everything was way back when everyone thought Lapsang Souchong was the exiled leader of Tibet and Woody Allen still made funny movies.

Knowstalgia

A trusty standby of a rant that essentially bemoans the fact that since they've stopped using slide rules and log tables in schools nobody seems to know very much at all, about anything, and especially about grammar and speling.

noosestalgia

A practice to be saved for the occasions when trapped in a social situation with anyone who wears their oh-so-pious left-wing conscience on their sleeve like a macaroon. The basic line you should adopt is that there was much less crime when, every now and again, someone got hanged.

Knorrstalgia

A light soufflé of a discussion centered on the fact that food tasted so much better in the old days when there were far fewer ingredients to choose from, and instead of things like balsamic vinegar you made do with that standard, industrial-strength brown stuff that made a salad reek like a fish factory, but taste like heaven, and the height of sophistication in the kitchen was the humble bouillon cube.

Nursestalgia

This is a train of thought that you will catch in your much later years when you find yourself sat up in bed on the receiving end of a particularly brusque bed-bath from a rather hefty-looking nurse who would obviously rather be doing something else. I mean, wasn't it supposed to be like that scene with Joanne Whalley in *The Singing Detective*?

Soixante-neufstalgia

This is a sordid and rather grubby form of nostalgia and I'm surprised at you for reading about it. It encompasses the erotic reverie that engulfs you when you get to pondering on just how much fun you had during your sexual canoodlings of yesteryear.

How to keep your partner on their toes

Take a new interest in your appearance. Buy and wear a new perfume or aftershave. Start going out a lot on your own for no apparent reason. Pretend to be happy.

But the age of romance needn't be dead—not when the romance of age can still burn bright

If you are in the fortunate position of still being with someone you love, then copy the following and mail it to them in a letter. Don't wait until it's too late to tell them what you feel. It's from Shakespeare's sonnets. And how wrong can you go with a Shakespeare sonnet?

> *To me, fair friend, you never*
> *can be old,*
> *For as you were when first*
> *your eye I ey'd,*
> *Such seems your beauty still.*

Three rather surprising but quite amusing things to try with your bus pass

1. Jimmying open the lock of someone's car

2. Trying to get an extra discount on crockery earthenware or clothing on the first day of the Macy's sale

3. Chopping up a line of talcum powder on a small mirror and offering it around as cocaine the next time those nicely turned-out Jehovah's Witnesses come round trying to save your soul

Aged provocateur

Victoria's Secret sells all manner of saucy lingerie to a discerning and playful clientele. Lace, frills, and straps all feature prominently, as does a gorgeously salacious touch of sleaze. Now if you're of the opinion that your days of even considering such accoutrements, let alone wearing them, are way behind you, think again.

After all, just because the present may have seen better days doesn't mean the wrapping paper can't still be fab. And what better way to signal to both yourself and your partner that sex is too much fun just to be left to the young. Indeed, even if you don't want to get into all the gloriously grubby sordidness that hanky-panky often involves, it's still worth buying a little something just to leave lying around inadvertently the next time your children come over for a visit.

It's amazing the things you can find shoved down the back of the closet

One of the most disquieting revelations that you can spring on your family is the fact that for most of your adult life you've suspected that you were gay. (Or, as the case may be, straight.) Such is the potency of this tactic that it really should only be deployed under specific, sensitive, and easily controlled circumstances. Personally I recommend Christmas dinner, just before the turkey is carved.

Nothing annoys like the noise of toys

When your children's children stop being babies they'll love nothing more than playing with toys that make a noise. And the noisier the noise, the better. Naturally, drums are a big hit, as are all manner of playthings that emit ear-piercing shrieks and wails or mind-numbing nursery rhyme tunes. Unsurprisingly, this behavior will drive their parents mad.

All of which really simplifies buying presents for your grandchildren come Christmas or on birthdays.

"How could you say that?"

When at your children's place having a meal with their friends it's always worthwhile dropping into any lull in the conversation an embarrassing anecdote about their behavior when they were little. Indeed the memory doesn't even have to be accurate, as you can always deny any denial they make by adding, "Well, you probably don't remember."

For example, "Oh, my little Johnny used to play with himself all the time when he was little" is always a winner.

LIFE IN THE SLOW LANE

Whenever you get in your car, wherever you're going, drive really slowly. When driving on a highway, drive in the far left lane and stick to the speed limit. After all, it is the law.

Life in the slow lane, two

Always remember to do your shopping on a Saturday. Use only the biggest of carts available. Place two, or at most three, small items in the cart. Then endeavor to block each aisle in turn by moving along it as slowly as possible, carefully scrutinizing the aisles of goods as you go. Every now and again suddenly stop your ambling and pick up some item for closer inspection. Also wander away from your cart frequently, ideally leaving it at right angles to the shelves. The busy intersections of aisles are also excellent places to position your cart to generate the maximum inconvenience. With but a little practice you should be able to pass a whole afternoon enjoyably in this way.

Why wait to lose your marbles when so much fun can be had by pretending to misplace them every now and again?

Need I say more?

The circular theory of eating out

When you're young and fancy going out for a meal, you find yourself drawn to loud, lively restaurants where you can hardly hear yourself think, let alone what the person next to you is saying. Then, as you get older, the very thought of eating out at such a place fills you with horror. Instead you choose restaurants where you don't feel boxed in, and conversation can ebb and flow without resorting to a megaphone. Then as advanced age creeps up on you, like a mugger in an underpass, one evening or lunchtime you will find yourself out for a meal and realize

that you have absolutely no interest
in anything anyone else is saying.
Indeed, if you do join in the conversation it's just out of politeness rather
than desire. And it's at this point
that you'll find that you've come full
circle and loud, lively restaurants
will suddenly start to appeal again.

Too many cooks

Next time you're visiting your children's home for a meal, offer to help with the cooking. Once your offer has been accepted there are many, many ways to have fun.

There's the "Oh, I thought you hadn't put the salt in yet" technique; the "Sorry, I thought it was on too high/too low" approach; and finally, the pièce de résistance that will truly brûlée their crèmes: "That's not the way to do it. Here, let me show you."

Drive them crazy

Another winning technique for use when at your children's house for a meal: After everyone's eaten, offer to help with the dishes. Then once everything is washed, put all the pots and pans and plates and dishes carefully away. In the wrong places.

The beauty of this tactic is that you'll be long gone from the scene of the crime when the irritation really kicks in.

SWEETS: THE BITTER TRUTH

All your grandchildren love you buying sweets, chocolates, or ice cream for them. But their parents would much prefer it if you didn't. Especially if you hand over said goodies just before mealtimes.

Act accordingly.

Cats 22

You'd have to be mad to want to live in a house with twenty-two cats. But if you did, then all kinds of fools would not bother knocking on your door. Like canvassing politicians, or oafs selling cleaning products, or those nicely suited shysters wondering if you're happy with your house alarm. You know, all those people with irritating sales pitches designed to drive you mad.

What I'm getting at is that maybe the best way to preserve your sanity is to occasionally feign a little madness. For instance, by living in a house with twenty-two cats.

Congratulations! You're a granddad/grandmother

A funny thing happens when your kids have kids. Suddenly you'll find yourself incredibly popular. Now it may well be because your children want you to share in the joy of their family life. Or it may be because they want a cheap baby-sitter.

You decide.

And while we're on the subject of baby-sitting

Of course, there are other reasons that you're popular as a baby-sitter for your grandchildren apart from the issue of cost. In the eyes of your children, unlike conventional baby-sitters, you're unlikely to raid the liquor cabinet, run up massive phone bills, or bonk your boyfriend on the sofa.

Which is all the more reason why you should do all three.

Deafinitely a winner

When out shopping pretend to be deaf. Keep repeating "Sorry?" and "You'll have to speak up." Eventually the unfortunate trying to communicate with you will end up bawling their head off just to get you to understand them. At this point affect a look of shock and rebuke them with the phrase, "You don't have to shout, I'm not deaf!"

EWB

There are many pivotal moments in history that divide the world into one state of affairs before the moment, and a significantly different one after it. For example, there's the moment when women first got the vote. Or the moment when Neil Armstrong first stepped on the moon. Or the moment when the Berlin Wall came down.

For the older person, sartorially speaking, there is a moment just as significant. That's the moment when the desire for comfort overrides the desire to look fashionable and you realize that Elasticized Waist Bands aren't such a bad idea after all.

Christmas or Christmiss?

As you get older your nearest and dearest will no doubt find it incumbent upon them to invite you over for Christmas. They could, of course, be doing this out of love and affection. However, they are much more likely to be doing it out of guilt. They can't bear the thought of your being alone at Christmas. Or, more accurately, they can't bear the thought of what people will think if they let you be alone at Christmas. So they invite you over.

The truly objectionable thing is that you're supposed to be grateful.

Grateful that you have to spend time in a house full of screaming kids. Grateful that you can't watch any of the TV programs you've been looking forward to seeing. Grateful for a lunch served so late that it's almost dinner. Grateful for having to eat brussels sprouts just to set your grand-children an example. Grateful for another pair of socks or another gift-pack of nauseatingly scented bath stuff. And grateful for being forced to confront just what a disappointing bunch of reprobates your family turned out to be.

My advice would be to feign illness. And make it something terribly infectious. Then call your loved ones with a list of the requirements you'll need while you're confined to your home, saying, in a rather pathetic voice, that you "haven't been able to make it to the shops." And to really pile on the guilt, add the phrase, "But don't worry about me, I'll be all right."

New from the makers of Viagra

Seeing as Viagra has been such a hit, maybe it's about time the manufacturers broadened their horizons?

Shyagra

For those who find themselves increasingly unwilling to meet new people as they get older

Tryagra

For those who become unwilling to try new things as they age

Dryagra

For those suffering from incontinence

Whyagra
For people unwilling to ask questions, especially of those in authority, like doctors

Fryagra
A truly remarkable drug that enables those with high blood pressure, heart problems, or cholesterol buildup to eat fried foods, including the glorious bacon-and-egg breakfast

Whyohwhyohwhyagra
For people who spend all their time asking questions on programs like *The View*

Niagra

For those having difficulty passing water

Piagra

For those who find it difficult, even under the most favorable of circum-stances, to divide the circumference of a circle by its diameter

Byebyeagra

For those who can't face the prospect of going to another funeral

Forget it

Many very clever people who've spent their lifetimes in academic institutions studying how the mind works have come to the conclusion that, on one level, you have to forget what you know in order to imagine something anew.

Surely in such a revelation about cognitive theory lies hope for us all. After all, forgetting what you know is one of the freebies that often accompany the aging process. So the more you forget the easier it should be for you to come up with new ideas, new solutions, and new designs for everything from cars to cupcakes to constitutional monarchies.

On "being a burden"

A lot of people as they get older worry that they "don't want to be a burden on their children in their old age." This is a shortsighted and foolish attitude. It is far more useful, productive, and appropriate to worry about not being enough of a burden on your children.

After all, weren't they a burden on you for long enough?

A few examples follow.

The burden of infirmity

Without a doubt this is the big one. It's the fear that as we age, something in our body, or our mind, will call "Time, gentlemen, please" ahead of schedule. Naturally you end up worrying, "Oh my God, who will look after me?"

But what you must never forget is that the fear is just as real for your children. Although they probably phrase it slightly differently. As in "Oh my God, I've got to look after them!"

So, in the words of another one of those irritating self-help manuals,

Feel the Fear and Do It Anyway. In other words, pretend to be infirm and watch the fun develop.

As an added bonus, seeing how your children react is a great way of deciding who gets what in the will.

A financial burden

This is the second pillar of burdenry. What you need to do is to let your offspring know that as your latter years approach you are somewhat devoid of savings. And pension plans. And financial sense.

Alternatively you can finesse the stress you engender by reassuring your children that you have provided for your old age by investing all your savings in undeniably sound ventures that promise excellent returns, for example, ostrich farms, Internet start-ups, or a vast array of "collector's item, limited-edition" plates issued by the Franklin Mint featuring "Kittens in a Kerfuffle."

That should put their minds at ease.

It's not just the secret of good comedy

The third key aspect of "being a burden" is timing. You must aim to reveal your problems at the time that will most inconvenience the plans and lives of your children. For example, a sudden attack of infirmity just before they're about to go away on vacation is always a winner. But the Holy Grail of the whole affair is to conjure up the prospect of a long-term, serious, and worsening condition at that moment when your children are thinking of moving.

A WORD OF WARNING

From this point on, death, The Big D, features heavily. If you are easily offended, it's probably best that you stop reading now. Mind you, if you are easily offended you probably stopped reading a long time ago.

Last words: a few first thoughts

Don't leave these to chance. Have something sorted out well in advance. Or you'll end up like Luther Burbank the famous horticulturist.* His last words were "I don't feel good." Accurate, but hardly profound.

The big problem is how do you know they're going to be your last words. What if you deliver your last line, then don't die? Do you hang around in silence? Or do you ask for that cup of tea or pillow, and run the risk of these becoming your last words?

*Oh, come on, everyone knows at least three famous horticulturists.

Your best bet is to choose something and have it written down somewhere. Or printed on a T-shirt. Or better still, tattooed on the inside of your left thigh.

Last words: a few second thoughts

Okay, so coming up with your own last words is no easy task. So to help inspire you I'll just mention the famous last words I've found most relevant, profound, and moving. They come from Conrad Hilton, the man who started with next to nothing and built the chain of hotels that bears his name. Just before he died he was asked if he had any last words of wisdom for the world. And he did: "Leave the shower curtain on the inside of the tub."

Now who could argue with that?

Preparing for the big day

Why should the people you leave behind have all the fun? They get to decide the date. They get to send out the invitations. They get to choose the music. They get to pick the food.

They even get to decide what handles to put on the coffin.

I mention the handles on the coffin thing because it was a choice I was confronted with when my father died. So there I was sitting in a gloomy office, still pretty much numb with shock, having to decide whether to go for the simple or the more rococo option handlewise. In the end we went for the simple brass handles.

And I found myself thinking the thought all of us comfort ourselves with in such circumstances: "It's what he would have wanted."

Only much later did I really think that line of reasoning through and come to the conclusion that I had no idea what "he would have wanted" for his own funeral. Maybe he didn't want something simple. Maybe he wanted to parade down the street behind a New Orleans marching band. Maybe he wanted that whole Dickensian deal with a top-hatted geezer leading two black-plumed horses. Or maybe he wanted to be buried in a field beneath an olive tree.

So to spare your nearest and dearest such dilemmas at what will necessarily be a somewhat fraught time in their lives, why not have the whole shebang sorted out well in advance? That way "what he/she would have wanted" will be abundantly clear because it will be down in black and white.

Now once you get your head around the concept of arranging your own funeral it is but a short step to realizing that, seeing as it is your last big party, why not have a little fun with it?

The Baroque Funeral

The Baroque Funeral is the full-on, over-the-top, Liberace-style affair. For this you need a hand-carved, completely gilded, mahogany coffin carried in by six large bodybuilders clad in flouncy Louis XV frippery, all crying. Atop the coffin should be a floral arrangement that stands taller than you (when you were still around to stand) and that should be based on some pretentious theme like "Truth and Beauty" or "The Good Samaritan" or "Celine Dion: Mad, Bad, or Just Plain Canadian?"

As the coffin is brought into the church—sorry, cathedral—a fanfare of trumpets should play your favorite Eminem song (I recommend "The Real Slim Shady") and a bejeweled midget should back away from it strewing rose petals in its path. The eulogy should be lifted from Shakespeare and be read by the likes of Sir Ian McKellen or Dame Judi Dench. And little girls dressed as Victorian shepherdesses should wander among the pews offering mourners silken handkerchiefs embroidered with a list of your achievements.

After the cremation, four Nubian warriors clad only in loincloths should arrive upon thoroughbred Arabian stallions to carry your ashes to the four corners of the globe. And as for

the catering back at the marquee,
start with individual Spam soufflés;
include at least one dish whose
ingredients have to be flown in from
abroad that very morning; and for
dessert hire Emeril Lagasse to weep
while handing out napkins and
reclining in a full-scale re-creation
of the Trevi Fountain made out of
both white and dark chocolate.

That should make the point.

The Minimalist Funeral

The Minimalist Funeral is somewhat of a contrast to the Baroque Funeral.

No coffin, just a body bag. No official cars, just complimentary one-day bus passes. No special music, just low, atonal humming. And no flowers, just the subtle suggestiveness of an elegantly lit empty vase.

As for the service/eulogy something along these lines will more than suffice:

"John Smith, born, lived, died, missed."

Back at the house toast and tap water should be more than enough to offer mourners.

The Slapstick Funeral

For this you need to choose and position your pallbearers very carefully. On one side of your coffin have very tall people, on the other side very short people. Replace the kneeling cushions in the church with whoopee cushions.

Request no flowers, but flour instead, and instruct the mourners to throw handfuls of the stuff at each other as the coffin passes. Employ a blubbering clown to patrol the aisles with a water pistol squirting water in the eyes of anyone not crying enough. And have the theme tune to *The Benny Hill Show* (the one where he chases scantily clad young girls at double speed) played as the coffin leaves the church.

At the reception lay on copious amounts of champagne in bottles that have been well and truly shaken up. And serve the drinks accompanied by large custard pies.

The Soap Opera Funeral

To carry this out successfully you need to get in touch with a theatrical agency and hire an actor. If you're a man, choose the most stunning-looking woman you can find and rent an all-black outfit that oozes sensuality with just a hint of wild sordidness. If you're a woman, you need to track down an actor who is honed, buffed, and more gorgeous looking than any mortal has the right to be. Then rent him tight black leather trousers, a clinging white T-shirt, and a large, throbbing motorbike.

Of course, it's vital that you tell nobody that you're doing any of this.

In fact, it's vital that the funeral carries on completely normally at all times. Until the right moment comes. Then as everyone is sitting down in the church or chapel or wherever, have your actor make their entrance. So the mysterious woman in black enters, walks up the aisle, places a single red rose and a pair of hand-cuffs on your coffin, then turns and walks away with a tear in her eye. The actor does the same, except he rides up on the motorbike.

Leave no explanation anywhere as to who these people are, or why they should be heartbroken at your demise.

The Surreal Funeral

Again no flowers. Instead ask for bouquets of fish. Instead of a eulogy arrange for an IRS agent to read a randomly chosen page from the Lands' End catalog. For the music get a string quartet of blind musicians to come in and tune their instruments. As for the coffin, have one made out of something soft and malleable like plasticine or something that will start to melt at room temperature like frozen Brie.

As a finishing touch, only invite people you never knew.

The Changing Tombs Funeral

Finally, why not save your relatives the stress of sorting out the whole affair by getting your neighbors to arrange your funeral with just a little help from Carole Smillie and Laurence Llewelyn-Bowen?

(Just a wild guess here, but you might well end up with a lilac coffin.)

But enough about funerals— instead let's just nail that one great last lie, you know, the one that says "You can't take it with you"

After your demise, arrange for all your assets to be turned into cash. Then arrange for the cash to line your coffin. Then specify cremation. But keep all this a secret from your family and friends until that moment when the coffin slides ever so serenely through those little curtains.

Well, they should all have been nicer to you when you were alive, shouldn't they?

OUTRODUCTION

I leave this to the words of John Webster,
the fifteenth-century English poet:

> *Is not old wine wholesomest, old*
> *pippins the toothsomest?*

> *Does not old wood burn brightest,*
> *old linen wash whitest?*

> *Old soldiers, sweetest, are surest,*
> *and old lovers soundest.*

But then again he died aged forty-two,
so what did he know?